Culture Without Accountability

WTF?

What's the Fix?

CULTURE WITHOUT ACCOUNTABILITY

WTF?

What's the Fix?

JULIE MILLER
BRIAN BEDFORD

Criffel Publishing

Austin, Texas

Published by
Criffel Publishing
Austin, Texas
www.millerbedford.com

Cover and text design by Bookwrights
ISBN 978-0-9898469-2-9

For our parents

Thanks for teaching us the importance of accountability.

We are forever grateful.

CONTENTS

FOREWORD

W hy did we feel compelled to write a book about accountability?

We think lack of accountability is a serious problem in the world today—and it's getting worse all the time. We are concerned that, if uncorrected, this trend will continue to have a negative effect on businesses, employees, families, and, in the end, the world we live in. We don't want to see that happen and we're passionate about fixing it!

First we couldn't help noticing all the issues we read about in the news, saw in our own community, and even experienced personally, as consumers. People these days want to blame others rather than being accountable when something goes wrong.

We paired this with the need for accountability we saw in the business world. Every time we worked with a client company in defining the business culture that would best support their strategies and help with their success, accountability was at the top of their list.

Accountability, or the lack of it, was a common theme everywhere we turned. However, the idea of writing a book seemed like such a huge undertaking and, quite honestly, not something we were very interested in doing. The fact that both of us are huge extroverts made this challenge an even greater one. The idea of sitting at a computer for many hours a day, churning through details and specific word choices, really had us running for the door!

However, our worldwide experience in multiple businesses has shown us that businesses that emphasize accountability are more successful businesses. This greater chance for success, and the fact that we like to address critical issues head-on, compelled us to ditch our fears and become part of the solution.

So, that's how this all began.

We understand that in our 24/7 world, everyone is under time constraints, and this is especially true for executives. That's why we made sure this book is a quick read—just right for a plane ride. More importantly, it provides a straightforward process for reinstating accountability in your business and, we hope, the world around us.

PART ONE

PART ONE

What's The Foundation?

If you could kick the person in the pants responsible for most of your trouble, you wouldn't sit for a month.

—Theodore Roosevelt

W e'd like to begin by telling you a story. This concerns a time when accountability made a difference in a situation in which we were involved. Recently, when we had a problem with travel, accountability effectively defused the situation. Here's what happened:

We were coming home from a Caribbean vacation, and we had a scheduled overnight stay in Dallas-Fort

Worth, since the connections wouldn't get us home in a single day. We got up the next morning to beautiful sunshine outside our hotel room window (always a good start for a travel day). Then, out of nowhere, came the mother of all hail storms. Green-black skies, battering hail, high winds. The works.

All air travelers know how this goes. One fifteen-minute delay leads to another, and before you know it, you've been waiting for hours. We changed gates seven times in all, and at one point we were actually allowed to board a plane. We thought for sure we were out of there—but not so. We learned that the planes on the ground during the hailstorm, including the one we were on, had to be checked for damage—which turned out to be extensive in some cases. So by now, you're beginning to comprehend the tension that was in the air that day. (Actually the airport; we were only hoping to get in the air!) We had been in the DFW airport all day, awaiting our short connecting flight home. Finally we boarded our second plane for home. Once the plane was fully boarded, the pilot came out of the cockpit to talk to us. Not a good sign. However, this is where the real story of accountability comes in. (Sorry for the long build-up, but scene-setting is key.)

The captain came out of the cockpit and looked us squarely in the eyes to share his news. He did not hide in the cockpit. Instead, he grabbed the flight attendants' public address system and stood in the middle of the aisle. This is our best recollection of what he said: "I have some good news and some bad news. The good news is, we will be getting you home tonight, I promise. The bad news is, it won't be on this aircraft." To which the crowd on board roared in disapproval.

He went on to say, "I will be walking down the aisle in order to give everyone a chance to take a swing at me, so get your purses, laptops, pillows, whatever you want, ready to swing. This is not the flight attendants' fault, so I hope you won't take it out on them. The buck stops with me, and I'll take the blame."

He asked us to please stay seated as the airline determined what gate we'd be departing from. "You've been through enough changes today," he said, "so I want to get it right. Meantime, let me tell you what's happened, and let me apologize. As we were doing the pre-flight checks onboard, we realized that the plane's tail number didn't match the tail number on the paperwork that I was given. As I researched further, I realized that this plane you are sitting on is due for inspection—NOW! You were boarded on the wrong plane, in other words. I am embarrassed for myself and my company, but as our customers, you deserve to know the truth."

Needless to say, we passengers were all astonished. What could customers do at that point? We had the truth, we had an apology, and soon we'd have a plane that would be taking us home. Yes, the day had been a total screw-up, but the situation had been defused. And to the captain's credit, he did walk the entire length of the plane, giving everyone a chance to ask questions or, as in our case, to congratulate him for having the integrity to come clean with the truth, and apologize.

By his actions and behavior, he was able to calm the passengers, protect his flight attendants, and restore respect for his company. No cover-up, no excuses, no lies! Isn't that the way things should be handled?

We like this story because it paints a realistic picture of what accountability can look like when done well, and it shows how anyone can make a huge difference just by choosing to handle a situation responsibly. Nine out of ten captains might have chosen to make a simple announcement from the cockpit rather than disclosing the whole truth. What made this captain handle it differently?

This story is a scene-setter for what we'll be discussing in the rest of the book. However, before we go further, let's get a common understanding of what we mean when we talk about accountability.

ACCOUNTABILITY DEFINED

So what is accountability? Some people might say that accountability is synonymous with blame. I'm "held accountable" means "I'm blamed."

Others use the terms *accountability* and *responsibility* interchangeably, but to us the two are not the same. Responsibility can denote ownership as in, "I'll handle that," or burden, as in, "I have the responsibility for this." We think of responsibility as being at the front end, clarifying who is doing what and who will be responsible, while accountability is a mindset at the back end—that is, after the fact. An accountable person owns up to the results, whether good or bad. So in this regard, someone can be responsible, but not accountable.

Here's a definition we came across in a video from the training company CRM Learning, called *Accountability That Works.*

Accountability – a personal willingness, after the fact, to answer for the results of your behaviors and actions

We really like this definition. Here's why.

Personal willingness – Personal means *me*, not someone else, but *me*... unmistakable. This doesn't mean *Blame someone else* or *Get a lawyer and sue someone*. Personal means *What did I have to do with this? What could I have done better?* No excuses!

We love the word **willingness** in the definition! Think about trying to convince someone to take ownership for a mistake. Isn't it easier if people own their own mistakes, and do so willingly?

After the fact – What better way to improve outcomes than by taking the time to seriously review our prior actions?

Answer for Results – After all, aren't *results* what businesses are seeking? If you don't have to be accountable for what you say you are going to do, then how will an organization succeed? Also, notice that we don't suggest getting grilled for results or hammered when you screw up. If you feel safe to talk to your manager about your results, and if you can honestly say what went well and what didn't, don't you think you will have a chance to learn from your mistakes and have a better outcome next time?

Behaviors and Actions – This is our favorite part of the definition! Behaviors and actions are what make all the difference. They are what can make an individual successful—or not—and they can make or break businesses, too. Behaviors are the things that people can hear us say or see us do. You did this, you said that—or you didn't. You alone are responsible for your actions. The good news is that you have the ability to change your behavior. How you act or what you do is not a given. If things are not going well, you have the choice to make corrections.

However, that takes us back to the notion of willingness. To change behavior, you have to want to do so. For example, your boss may point out that you tend to talk over others when you're making a point in meetings, and you don't listen well to what others are saying. But even your boss can't make you change your behavior; he or she can only point out what would make you more successful.

You have to be willing to make the changes. That choice is up to you.

Why The Fuss?
WHY IS ACCOUNTABILITY AN ISSUE?

*The right thing to do and the hard thing to do are
usually the same.*

—Steve Maraboli, *Life, the Truth, and Being Free*

Have you noticed that shirking responsibility for one's actions is becoming the rule rather than the exception? We noticed a decline in accountability all around us, and it scared us into writing this book.

Sadly, we've all witnessed terrible examples in many different organizations and industries: sports, politics, financial institutions, businesses, the entertainment industry, churches, schools, even in parenting. But before we share examples, one point we'd like to make is that we recognize that human beings—ourselves included—are complicated and flawed. At one time or another we're all guilty of making bad choices or using poor judgment. Sometimes circumstances cause us not to live up to our own expectations of ourselves, and sometimes we do what we think is the right thing at the time, but events prove that it wasn't the right thing after all.

So when we use examples of people behaving without accountability, our purpose is not to be judgmental. It is to show the problems that these chosen behaviors cause—and the fallout that follows. We'd like to point out how much better life is when we can rely on people to behave in an accountable fashion and to be role models for others.

Some of these stories are so widely known that we can merely mention them without details and you will know the scandal attached. Many sports, for example, face the issue of performance-enhancing drugs. Think how many times you've heard, "I have never knowingly taken performance-enhancing drugs." Cycling is infamous for Lance Armstrong, Floyd Landis, and many others, all of whom protested their innocence until finally they were forced to admit that they had doped. Doping was an issue in other sports, too: baseball makes you think of Barry Bonds and Mark McGwire. Track and field brings to mind the ignominy of Ben Johnson and Marion Jones. And we all know countless other examples.

In politics, consider Anthony Weiner (pun acknowledged), the former U.S. representative from New York who denied sending racy photos of himself to women over the Internet, but later admitted to having done exactly that. Probably the most extreme example is John Edwards. While seeking the nomination for U.S. president, Edwards denied having fathered an illegitimate child, and even went so far as to persuade one of his aides to falsely claim that he was the father. Eventually, though, the truth came out; indeed it was Edwards' baby.

The list goes on: Financial Institutions (Lehman Brothers, Barclays), big business (BP, Tyco, Enron), religion (the Roman Catholic Church), entertainment (Arnold Schwarzenegger and a cast of thousands), colleges (none worse than Penn State University). We could go on, but we want you to keep reading rather than locking yourself in your room in despair.

Lack of accountability isn't unique to large institutions or industries. It exists because individuals make bad decisions, or exercise poor judgment, and then fail to take responsibility for what they've done. Their decisions are major blunders, but even worse is what these individuals choose to do next. Too often they spend all their energy, resources, and influence trying to cover up, to dodge the consequences of their decisions.

When individuals in leadership make bad decisions, the culture of the organization or institution can be affected—and this impact can stretch into the future. The actions of a few can lead to the demise of the institution and the end of careers—the leaders' own and those of their employees. Just think of Kenneth Lay and Jeffrey Skilling, former CEOs of Enron, whose actions resulted in disastrous consequences, both for their own company, and for Enron's auditing firm, Arthur Andersen, as well as for all employees of both companies. Lay's and Skilling's roles in the scandal of corporate abuse and accounting fraud led to the downfall of Enron and the dissolution of Arthur Andersen.

In a sense, parents can also be thought of as leaders. They are the leaders of their families, the ones responsible for teaching their children to do the right thing, and to develop into mature adults who are accountable for their actions, and for how they function in society.

We appeal to parents, business leaders, politicians, sports figures, and people in charge of major institutions to help reverse the trend of this lack of accountability. Without action, things won't change—and they're apt to even get worse.

Why do you think so many people remain unaccountable for their actions? The reason is that being accountable, as well as holding other people accountable, is really, really hard. Without a culture or a process that encourages this behavior, it won't happen. Letting things slide, taking the soft option, hiding the truth, being less than entirely honest—these things make up the path of least resistance, which always seems easier at first. Being accountable, by contrast, requires toughness and strength of character.

When something goes wrong in a business, the worst thing to do is to try and cover it up, because when the truth is revealed (and the truth almost always comes out), the impact is worse than it would have been if the person had owned up in the first place.

Institutions that get caught after covering up egregious behavior are levied more severe penalties than those that didn't attempt a cover-up.

Consider seven-time winner of the prestigious Tour de France, cyclist Lance Armstrong. He insisted for more than a decade that he was innocent of doping, and he even went so far as to sue people who dared suggest he wasn't entirely clean. And what did his actions cost him? Armstrong finally admitted he'd doped. As a result, he's been stripped of his seven Tour de France wins, he's forever banned from competing, and he's lost millions of dollars in endorsements. In addition, he has spent millions on litigation, the consequences of which may cost him many more millions in restitution. Finally, of course, there's the matter of his shattered reputation. Was his lack of accountability worth it?

In this book, our aim is to get you upset about the lack of accountability in the world, and enlist you to do what you can to change the trend. We hope to convince you that it's worth the time and effort it would take to instill accountability in your business, your school, your community, and yes, your family. Maybe because you are reading this book, you already feel compelled to address the problem, but you don't know how to go about it. Later in these pages we will help you with that by sharing the benefits of a culture of accountability, and we'll provide you with a proven process for how to make that happen.

What're The Fundamentals?

How Do We Learn to Be Accountable?

*Parents can only give good advice or put [their children]
on the right paths, but the final forming of a person's
character lies in [one's] own hands.*

—Anne Frank

Accountability is not something people are born with. There isn't an accountability gene that some people have and others don't. Rather, accountability is something we learn from our parents, teachers, friends, employers, and role models. It's a mindset that compounds over the years, as we are faced with more and more complex situations in our lives, resulting in more difficult choices and decisions.

So it's not surprising that, when we've asked people when they first learned about accountability, most talk about lessons their parents taught them. Parents should instill a set of values and, based upon those values, some behaviors are understood to be acceptable, and others unacceptable. Learning which is which allows us to choose how we are going to behave and this, in turn, affects how we are perceived by others.

A few common values that children learn from parents are:

- Treating others with respect
- Saying "Please" and "Thank You"
- Learning the difference between right
    and wrong
- Telling the truth
- Accepting responsibility for our actions
- Admitting when we make a mistake
- Learning to apologize

Effective parents teach us that we will be held accountable to those values. They praise us when we do right, and they punish us when we don't. We learn about accountability through increasing levels of responsibility, such as participating in household chores. It might begin when a child picks up his toys, cleans her room, does the dishes, or takes out the trash. Over time accountability grows more complex: mowing the grass, choosing to do homework, making good grades, abiding by curfew. Getting kids to accomplish these tasks isn't always easy. It usually takes more effort for parents to make the child do the chore than it would for the parents to do it themselves. But when a child completes chores in a way that satisfies his or her parent, the result is higher self-esteem on the part of the child. The child becomes accustomed to meeting other people's expectations. This becomes increasingly important when the child starts school and has to meet the expectations of a teacher.

Author Kay Wills Wyma, in her book, *Cleaning House: A Mom's 12-Month Experiment to Rid Her Home of Youth Entitlement*, writes:

> I came to realize that not one of my five children knew how to do their own laundry. Not one could clean a bathroom—I mean really clean it. Not one could cook, serve, and clean up after a full dinner. I wasn't sure my

eight-year-old could even cut his waffles... they'd been getting a sweet free ride, especially in their home life. With me stepping in and doing for them—rarely, if ever, putting genuine responsibilities on their plate—they didn't have a chance to realize their potential... When I step in, fix [my children's] problems, and do those little household chores (or homework!), I send the message that they *can't* do it themselves. And if they can't do the small things, how will they ever attempt the big things?

We don't think the realization that provoked Wyma's 12-month experiment is very different from the dynamic in many families these days. Parents want what is best for their children; however, their approach may not be yielding the long-term results they desire. This, coupled with the messages kids are getting from celebrities and sports heroes, often fails to stress the importance of personal accountability.

Our friends with younger children have brought up the common practice of giving all the kids trophies for *playing* a sport, not for *winning* the event. No, winning isn't everything, but are we preparing our children for the real world when (with all good intentions) we obstruct their learning the difference between defeat and victory and how to handle either with grace? It is a lot easier to handle large-scale disappointments and setbacks in life if you have successfully managed bumps in the road during childhood. Rather than preparing our children for life, are we instead protecting them and failing to provide them the tools they will need later?

To hold someone accountable is to apply consequences until the desired behavior is achieved. We understand that this is really hard, which is where parental fortitude comes in. It takes effort for the parent to hold the child accountable. But without that effort, the child may win the everyday battle, but lose the war in life.

As we get older, we become accountable to people other than family members: teachers, coaches, family friends, scout leaders. At this point, away from our family unit, we have to start using our own judgment about what we are and are not accountable for, because the standards to which outsiders hold us may differ from those of our family members.

As learning continues, we may become accountable to an employer or a boss. This helps us learn different perspectives, broadens our base of experience, and increases our knowledge. A boss may set different standards, and we have to adapt if we want to be successful. Occasionally a boss may ask us to do things that don't fit with our values, at which point we have to make the choice whether this is the right place for us to work. Conversely, good leaders help make us better individuals by guiding us to higher levels of integrity and accountability. Whom we choose as role models can have a significant impact on our future.

Our friend Anne heads a very successful bank in Dallas. Recently we were talking about the stereotype of the modern kid now graduating from college. Many have never held down jobs, and they've had much in life given to them without their working for it. We asked Anne how these kids do when they enter the workplace, and she said, "I have no idea! We don't hire them!"

The cycle continues. The next stage comes when we establish long-term relationships with a spouse or partner. Now we're not making choices with only ourselves in mind; our choices have significant impact on our spouse. What may be best for me may not be best for him or her, and vice versa. How do we make choices that nurture the relationship, while at the same time being accountable to ourselves?

And then if we have children of our own, or achieve positions of responsibility wherein people report to us, the learning compounds yet again—only this time it's *our* job to set standards and teach others the importance of being accountable.

True accountability is not just about making the right choices, or doing the right thing, it's our willingness, after the fact, to answer for the results of our actions. All the parenting we receive, our life experiences, and everything we've learned can give us direction, but in truth, the ultimate choice is always ours. What kind of person do we want to be? How do we choose to behave? Are we going to take responsibility for our actions, or cover up the facts and look for someone else to blame when something goes wrong? Will we choose to do the right thing even when no one is watching? After all, this is the ultimate test of accountability!

PART TWO

What're The Facts?

The Good, the Bad, and the Ugly about Accountability

The Good: Accountability Done Well

If you are more interested in being liked and popular than holding people accountable for results, you have a serious leadership weakness. It is not your job to make people happy. Your job is to get them better...

—Dave Anderson, *No Nonsense Leadership*

I t's not that easy to find examples of accountability done well. Why? We guess that when people do the right thing, it's just not newsworthy. When there's a big issue, the mere willingness to tell the truth puts out the flames that can get fanned by lies and cover-ups. Deceit breeds public interest, which builds outrage and gets people firing up their Twitter accounts. By contrast, telling the truth takes away the drama. With transparency, people understand the story is over, and what could have been a contentious situation can be defused.

When situations arise in which you're at fault, make an error in judgment, or let others down, you have a choice about how you respond. Simply saying, "I'm sorry" goes a long way toward calming matters. As soon as you realize you've made a mistake, you have the power to shape the way you are viewed by others.

Here's an example that clearly illustrates how integrity in a bad situation can influence the way others see you.

On June 2, 2010, Detroit Tiger Armando Galarraga was pitching a perfect game—something that has only happened twenty times since 1880. Then, in what should have been the final out of the game, Umpire Jim Joyce ruled Cleveland Indians runner Jason Donald safe, thus ruining Galarraga's perfect game.

Needless to say, the situation got plenty of media

attention. Amy K. Nelson of ESPN wrote about the incident on ESPN.com, in a piece she called "Searching for meaning in the mistake" (capitalization hers): "... As Joyce runs off the field, Tigers veteran manager Jim Leyland approaches Joyce. 'Jimmy!' Leyland barks. 'You blew it! You blew it, go look at the video!'..."

After viewing the postgame replay, Joyce realized that Leyland was right. Joyce had blown it. That safe should have been called an out. The umpire was beside himself.

Nelson continues...

He chooses to give the media rare access to the umpires' locker room. He takes full responsibility for kicking the call. When the media leave, Leyland comes in for a beer. He tells Joyce that he blew the call and that he needs to move past it. Tigers' general manager Dave Dombrowski visits, too, concerned for Joyce's well-being. Both men have known Joyce for decades and, like the players in the league who voted him the top umpire in an ESPN The Magazine poll, hold enormous respect for him.

Joyce appreciates the gestures, but his mind

is on one person. He asks Dombrowski whether he can talk to Galarraga.

Dombrowski leaves, and a few minutes later he returns to the umpires' room with the 28-year-old pitcher from Venezuela. Galarraga walks up to Joyce and while hugging him says, "We are all human." Joyce, crying, apologizes in English and Spanish and then leaves the room, unable to speak.

...But an e-mail to Jim Joyce from Mark Wunderlich, another veteran NBA ref, is one of the most compelling. He wrote, "I have admired your work for years and I have been thinking about you the last couple of days... It shall pass and the only thing people will remember is the class you showed during this time. From one professional to another, I'm proud of you, Buddy."

What an act of accountability and integrity. Imagine for a moment that Jim Joyce had tried to justify the call, or even gone quietly on his way, hoping all would be forgotten. You know that call wouldn't have been forgotten. The next time Joyce was calling a game in Detroit, or anywhere for that matter, he probably would have been booed out of the ballpark. Instead, he's viewed as a regular human being, just like the rest of us. Capable of making mistakes, but also big enough to admit his errors and apologize. That simple gesture of integrity seems brave, and it shows the world what Jim Joyce is made of!

WHEN BEING ACCOUNTABLE IS GOOD FOR THE ENTIRE ORGANIZATION

Let's consider the February 15, 2012, student arrests at Texas Christian University in Fort Worth, Texas. This story hit close to home with us, because Julie grew up in Fort Worth, and she earned her Master's degree from TCU.

In case you didn't follow the story, here's what happened. Eighteen students at TCU were arrested as a part of a six-month drug sting. Seventeen were caught making "hand-to-hand" sales of marijuana, cocaine, ecstasy, and prescription drugs (including Xanax, hydrocodone, and others similar to OxyContin).

To put this in perspective, TCU is a relatively small private university. As we write this, the university has about 9500 students, and employs just under 2000 people. TCU has always been viewed as a tight-knit campus with a family atmosphere. It's a campus where students and faculty know and respect one another. So you can imagine the shock that went through the school, as well as through the Fort Worth community, when this news broke.

In response, Victor J. Boschini, Jr., TCU Chancellor, wrote the following letter as a way of announcing the sting to the campus. The letter was released on the morning the arrests were made.

Dear Campus Community,

Early today the Fort Worth Police Department and TCU Campus Police concluded an investigation into drug selling on and around campus that, unfortunately, led to the arrest of many current TCU students.

While this news is certainly shocking and disappointing, it is important to remember that TCU has clear expectations for its students: that they behave in an ethical manner, abide by campus policies and adhere to state and federal law. These students are charged with acting in a manner that is incompatible with TCU values and against the law. That is simply unacceptable and such reported behavior is not tolerated at this University.

We have a responsibility to ensure that our campus environment is free of such behavior. Today's actions highlight that responsibility. The students involved were immediately separated from TCU and criminally trespassed from campus. Further, according to University policy, students arrested and found in violation of distributing drugs are subject to immediate expulsion from TCU.

TCU has never before experienced a magnitude of student arrests such as this. In fact, Campus Police records show only five student arrests related to drug law violations in recent years. I have asked our vice chancellor for student affairs, Dr. Kathy Cavins-Tull, to examine whether any new programs or procedures need to be implemented to curtail this type of behavior in the future. The Fort Worth Police Department also has offered to help in these efforts.

Today's events have forever changed the lives of the involved students, and we hope they will find a healthy way to move forward. Also, the next couple of weeks will be tough for the TCU family. There is no doubt that it will hurt to see our name associated with this type of behavior. But we must not allow this moment to define us. We must remember that we are overwhelmingly a community of dedicated students, faculty and staff and focused on changing the world through our collective work and commitment to leadership.

Sincerely,

Chancellor Victor J. Boschini, Jr.

Most disturbing was that included in the number arrested were four members of the highly acclaimed football team. In a statement sent out by TCU, Gary Patterson, the Head Coach of TCU's football program, remarked:

There are days people want to be a head football coach, but today is not one of those days. As I heard the news this morning, I was first shocked, then hurt, and now I'm mad. Under my watch, drugs and drug use by TCU's student-athletes will not be tolerated by me or any member of my coaching staff, period. I believe strongly that young people's lives are more important than wins or losses. Our program is respected nationally for its strong ethics and, for that reason, the players arrested today were separated from TCU by the university.

There was no cover-up - The University officials and TCU police cooperated fully with the Fort Worth Police department. Both leaders in the organization were accountable to the university that employs them. But most importantly, they held the students accountable for their actions by applying consequences for those actions.

Consistency - If you're in charge, it's very important that you apply consequences consistently. You can't hold some accountable and make allowances for others. There is no place for favoritism in a healthy business or institution.

To illustrate, here's another story from TCU, the second chapter in the Gary Patterson/ Chancellor

Boschini story. In October 2012, just a few months after the sting and arrests and expulsions, TCU's starting quarterback, Casey Pachall, was arrested for DWI. There were higher stakes for the football team this time, because the next quarterback in line was a redshirt freshman with very limited playing time. It would mean serious consequences for the whole football team if Pachall couldn't play. But what message would it send if Pachall *were* allowed to play? Driving while intoxicated is serious. So what was the right thing, both for the student and for the university?

As reported by Stefan Stevenson in the *Fort Worth Star Telegram* on October 10, 2012:

> Patterson had a lengthy meeting with Pachall and his parents to discuss the situation. Patterson also met with Chancellor Victor Boschini and Athletic Director Chris Del Conte. The end result was a mutually agreed upon decision by Patterson, Boschini, Del Conte, Pachall and his parents. Pachall withdrew from school and entered an in-patient substance abuse program. Pachall can enroll in the spring and rejoin the team if he gets clean and if he has demonstrated that he has changed.

Patterson said, "It was important for me he knew he had an opportunity to come back here. You have to have hope in what you do."

"What we're saying is, the health and the safety of the student-athlete is the first priority," Boschini said. "I'm happy to support Coach Patterson's decision because what I think his decision says is we're walking the walk and talking the talk."

Patterson said, "We're trying to help [Pachall] with his life. Period... For all those of you who always think it's always about wins and losses – wrong."

TCU's website states:

Our Mission

To educate individuals to think and act as ethical leaders and responsible citizens in the global community

Our Vision

To be a world-class, values-centered university

Words like this do not have any value if they are not backed up with actions. How would these words have been perceived if the aforementioned incidents had been handled differently? How do you think the community feels about Chancellor Boschini and Coach Patterson, based upon the accountability they both took for themselves and demanded of others? Do you think their stock has gone up in the community? You bet it has. They let us know that the values described on the TCU website are not empty words. Rather, they have meaning, and they guide the actions and behaviors of the people leading the institution.

Compare this to the actions of Jim Tressel, former coach at Ohio State University, who failed to report violations by his players to school officials—violations including allegations of receiving cars, cash, and other benefits from boosters or trustees. Initially, the coach lied, saying that he was unaware of violations in his program. Later, he acknowledged that he had known about them.

Let's look at another example. To us, one of the most memorable displays of accountability took place more than thirty years ago. The Tylenol recall is probably still taught in business schools as an example of how to handle a situation that could destroy a brand and the company that owns it. If you recall, around September 29, 1982, seven people from the Chicago,

Illinois, area died after taking potassium cyanide-laced capsules of the over-the-counter pain reliever Extra-Strength Tylenol.

Early in the investigation, sabotage during production was ruled out, and the authorities came to believe that the perpetrator had entered various stores, removed packages of Tylenol from the shelves, laced their contents with solid cyanide compound at another location, and then replaced the bottles.

Johnson & Johnson warned hospitals and distributors and also halted Tylenol production and advertising. On October 5, less than a week later, Johnson & Johnson issued a nationwide recall of Tylenol products; an estimated 31 million bottles were in circulation at the time, with a retail value of more than U.S. $100 million. When it was determined that only capsules were tampered with, the company offered to exchange all Tylenol capsules already purchased by the public for solid tablets.

In a *New York Times* article published on March 23, 2002, Judith Rehak wrote:

...[It was] predicted that the Tylenol brand, which accounted for 17 percent of the company's net income in 1981, would never recover from the sabotage. But only two months later, Tylenol was headed back to the market, this time in tamper-proof packaging and bolstered by an extensive media campaign. A year later, its share of the $1.2 billion analgesic market, which had plunged to 7 percent from 37 percent following the poisoning, had climbed back to 30 percent... James Burke, the company's chairman, was widely admired for his leadership in the decision to pull Tylenol capsules off the market, and for his forthrightness in dealing with the media... These moves were costly. Johnson & Johnson spent more than $100 million for the recall and re-launch of Tylenol [that year]... But Johnson & Johnson's shareholders were hurt only briefly. In 1982, the stock, which had been trading near a 52-week high just before the tragedy, see-sawed in panic selling but recovered to its highs only two months later.

In our opinion, this was nothing short of miraculous. Moreover, Tylenol made a hero of Johnson & Johnson.

How easy would it have been for Burke to say, "This is a terrible thing that has happened, but it is not our fault the Tylenol was tampered with." Or he could have passed the blame to the stores, "The stores allowed this perpetrator to re-stock these, so it's their fault!"

But what good would that have done? The consumers would have completely lost faith in the Tylenol brand, regardless of who was at fault, and Johnson & Johnson would have been the biggest loser of all. The business could have gone down the drain, and Johnson & Johnson could have consoled itself by saying, "It wasn't our fault!" Instead, company leaders were able to counter with actions that saved not only their reputation, but also their business. Their behavior cemented a positive perception in the minds of consumers.

So what are we trying to get across with these examples? Why do we keep saying that businesses should apply consequences to those who choose inappropriate behavior? We know it appears easier at first to try to hide the truth and walk away from difficult situations. As we've already established, this is a very human response. No one wants to make mistakes or be subjected to ridicule for being caught doing something wrong. However, making the wrong choice after things have gone off track only makes the situation worse. If you make the right decision in the aftermath of mistakes, your stock can actually go *up* in the view of others. Telling the truth is good for your personal image, and it's good for business. Because of TCU's actions, parents surely felt confident that the leaders of the university were doing their best to provide the right environment for students. Similarly, Johnson & Johnson's actions helped restore consumer trust and enabled a viable business to carry on bringing the world great products.

Are there commonalities in these examples of people behaving with accountability? Why did the umpire Jim Joyce choose to apologize directly to Armando Galarraga, when it would have been easier to issue an apology via the media? Why did TCU coach Gary Patterson behave as he did? Both of these individuals had the courage to tell the truth, to accept responsibility, and to act with integrity. Our bet is that they were taught the importance of accountability in their early years, so that later behaving in an accountable fashion was vitally important to them.

THE BAD: ACCOUNTABILITY DONE POORLY

A body of men holding themselves accountable to nobody ought not to be trusted by anybody.

—Thomas Paine

It's easy to find examples of individuals, companies, and even governments that behave without accountability, and then make matters worse by attempting a cover-up. Is this behavior more prevalent today than it was, say, fifty years ago? Or is it simply the influence of the Internet that makes information instantly available around the world? Whatever the answer, one thing is clear—today a wrongdoer is much more likely to get caught for all the world to see. So beyond the moral imperative to accept responsibility, there's a practical imperative. We believe it's better to accept the short-term pain, "'fess up," and give yourself a chance to recover.

When individuals act without accountability and get caught, the damage is primarily to themselves and their personal legacy, although clearly their families (and also fans, in the case of sports stars) are damaged as well. When big organizations with people in positions of power and influence do the same thing, the damage can be much more widespread. Two examples illustrate this point.

First, consider the 1989 soccer disaster in Hillsborough, England. Described by the U.K. media as the "biggest cover-up in U.K. history," it involved the deaths of 96 soccer fans, and injuries to hundreds more, at the semi-final of a major soccer competition in Sheffield, England. Not only did all the organizations involved refuse to be held accountable, but also they actively conspired to cover up their failures by falsifying documents, and placing the blame on innocent fans.

Here's how it went down: The semi-final match of the 1989 Football Association Cup competition was scheduled for April 15, 1989, pitting the Liverpool Football Club against the Nottingham Forest Football Club. These were two very successful and well-supported teams. The semi-finals are always staged in neutral stadiums, to ensure that no one has a home advantage, and on this occasion Sheffield's Hillsborough stadium was selected as the neutral venue. There had been problems with overcrowding at this stadium before, both in 1981 and in 1988, when it was chosen as a semi-final venue. Many people were injured on both occasions, but the 1989 semi-final match went forward even though, following the previous incidents, many recommendations for stadium improvements had been ignored.

Liverpool fans had already been involved in a previous disaster, in the Heysel Stadium in Brussels, on May 29, 1985, when Liverpool fans broke through a barrier and attacked the fans of Juventus of Turin. As the Juventus fans tried to escape, a retaining wall collapsed. Thirty-nine Juventus fans were killed, and 600 people were injured.

At that time, there were metal fences around the playing area. These fences were designed to prevent crowds from invading the playing surface known as "the pitch." Such invasions were frequent in the 1980s. The fences were successful in preventing pitch invasions, but they gave no avenue for escape in case an area became jammed with people. Therefore, in the event of overcrowding, people could be crushed. To complicate matters further, some areas of the stadium were for standing only, with no limit on the number of people allowed into the area. These standing areas, known as "pens," were especially dangerous, because the only way out was back the way you came in.

In the Hillsborough disaster, a dangerous crowd build-up began outside the stadium, because the entrances were inadequate to process the number of late-arriving fans trying to get in. In response, the local police—who were responsible for crowd management—ordered exit gates to be opened as a way of relieving pressure. This allowed fans to enter the stadium, but there was no control to let them know which direction to go. In previous years, entrances to the pens had been controlled and fans redirected when the pens were full, but on this occasion, no such controls were in place. The incoming fans poured into an already overcrowded area, and there was no way out, so those coming in crushed the first arriving fans against the metal barriers at the front. Ninety-six people lost their lives that day, and hundreds more were injured.

Even after the scale of the problem was recognized, emergency services were slow to respond, medical teams were not called until it was too late, and it is now estimated that many of those who died might have survived had medical attention been available earlier.

There were three groups responsible for this tragedy: the owners of Hillsborough stadium who ignored recommendations for stadium safety; the police who were responsible for crowd management and control; and the medical services workers who responded to the crisis. All these groups had their share of accountability for the disaster. However, instead of behaving accountably, the three groups blamed Liverpool fans for causing the problem. Because of that earlier disaster in Brussels, Liverpool fans were an easy target.

Not until 2012, after a detailed official report (the *Hillsborough Independent Report*), and the release of documents not previously available, did the true story emerge.

This is it: The stadium owners, who refused to accept that there were safety issues with the stadium, said the police had the responsibility to ensure safety. The truth, though, was that the owners didn't want to accept the cost of making changes to the stadium, despite issues of safety in previous years.

The emergency services tried to prove that the fans were drunk, even to the extent of taking blood alcohol measurements from all the deceased, and officials altered reports written at the time to avoid any suggestion that a better and faster response might have saved lives. Yet the 2012 report of the disaster said that as many as 41 of the 96 fatalities might not have occurred had the response been better.

As for the police, the 2012 report found that 164 original witness statements were altered to remove such words as "chaos," "panic," and any criticism of senior officers' actions, and a further 110 statements were removed altogether. One of the senior police officers conspired to shift all the blame onto the Liverpool fans by giving a false story, publicly, that Liverpool fans were drunk, arrived late without tickets, and forcibly broke into the stadium. This police misinformation produced press coverage that laid all blame for the disaster on Liverpool fans. The 2012 report revealed that the police had been instructed by higher-ups to prepare a "rock-solid story," and to put all the blame on "drunken, ticketless fans." It was subsequently—and officially—revealed that crowd behavior was not a contributing factor.

Worst of all was the impact on the families of the dead, who have had to listen for more than twenty years to stories about how the fans were responsible for their own deaths. The 2012 report gave great credit to the honesty, integrity, and perseverance of the families of the dead who have fought for justice for more than two decades. If only those responsible had acknowledged their own errors rather than trying to deflect blame, all this unnecessary guilt and anguish might have been avoided.

Instead, the original inquest verdict, "accidental death," has now been quashed, and a new criminal investigation will take place.

The second example we'd like to share is the scandal involving expense claims filed by Members of the Houses of Parliament in the U.K. In connection with this scandal, many individual reputations and careers were shattered, as was the confidence of the U.K. population in their government.

Members of both Houses of Parliament—the House of Commons and the House of Lords—are allowed to claim expenses "wholly, exclusively, and necessarily incurred for the performance of Parliamentary duties." Members represent constituencies all over the U.K., but they are required to be present at Parliament in London, so obviously there will be expenses—travel and accommodation, for example—involved.

There had been rumors for years that many members, up to and including senior ministers, were in the habit of submitting excessive and fictitious claims in order to pad their income. The House of Commons authorities, instead of admitting to the fact that there were serious issues of abuse and dealing with them, did their best to block any publication of information, even going so far as to put a motion to the House that would have exempted the disclosure altogether. Finally the authorities agreed to publish details of expenses, but with "sensitive information" (names, for example) removed.

Then in 2009, a full and uncensored copy of the expenses was leaked to a major U.K. newspaper, the *Daily Telegraph*, which began publishing details on a regular basis. The U.K. public was horrified at the extent of this abuse of privilege; they were appalled to see members of all parties and at all levels with their "noses in the trough." Some of the more egregious examples included expense claims for non-existent properties, claims for second homes already rented out, and—the one that perhaps irritated the public most—a claim for cleaning out a moat!

In this classic example of officials' not being accountable for their actions, those entrusted with the government of the country, representatives elected to look after the interests of the people who voted for them, *these* are the ones who betrayed the public trust.

The scandal dragged on for months, with many of the guilty initially denying any fraudulent activity. After the full truth was revealed, some members were prosecuted and sentenced to jail terms, others fired, and still others resigned or retired in disgrace.

How much better would this situation have been with a firm up-front response that included full disclosure, an admission of wrong-doing, and a commitment to fix the problem? Instead, the public was treated to a "slow drip" of tawdry details and months of negative publicity resulting in further distrust.

So what are the common traits of the individuals who denied accountability in our examples? It seems to us that people generally know the difference between right and wrong, and yet in both of these cases, people in power chose to be dishonest or deceptive. In the Hillsborough incident, they knew they'd made a mistake and they were afraid of getting caught. They knew that what they were doing was wrong but they were hoping they could get away with it. It takes courage to admit you made a mistake, and in these situations, the individuals took the cowardly option.

In the case of the U.K. Parliament, maybe the entitlement culture drove their choices: "Everyone else is doing it, so I'm entitled, too." This is not a good excuse, but without a culture of accountability, good people who know right from wrong can come to feel comfortable making bad choices.

Where was the system that should have provided incentives to do the right thing? These individuals were aware that they were not doing right, but they still made that choice. We must put systems in place that will drive people to make the right choices.

THE UGLY: WHAT DOES THE LACK OF ACCOUNTABILITY COST US?

*It is not only what we do, but also what we do not do,
for which we are accountable.*

—Moliere, 17th-century French playwright

What does *not* holding people accountable really cost us? In some cases, nothing. Sometimes, it's just a matter of how you could have offered some helpful counsel but didn't—no big deal. In other cases, not holding people accountable can have serious ramifications.

Consider the very public sex abuse scandal at Penn State University which broke in 2011. Wasn't the lack of accountability in this situation epic? To review the facts: This scandal involved football assistant coach Jerry Sandusky's sexual assault of boys, and the actions by very senior university officials to ignore the incidents—for years! In an independent investigation commissioned by the Board of Trustees of Penn State, and conducted by former FBI director Louis Freeh, it was found that Graham Spanier, the PSU President, and Joe Paterno, the football coach, along with athletic director Tim Curley and university vice-president Gary Schultz, all knew, as early as 1998, about allegations of Sandusky's child abuse, and all were complicit in failing to disclose them. Freeh stated that the four men had "failed to protect against a child sexual predator harming children for over a decade" and "empowered" Jerry Sandusky to continue his abuse. The report also blamed the trustees for fostering a "football first" atmosphere and for failing to create "a 'tone at the top' environment wherein Sandusky and other senior university officials believed they were accountable to it."

The costs in this situation were extremely high. Let's see how the costs piled up.

- Penn State spent $6.5 million on the independent inquiry.
- Sandusky was convicted of 45 counts, and sentenced to 60 years in prison.
- Shultz and Curley were indicted.
- Spanier and Paterno were fired by the University.
- The NCAA levied the following sanctions:
  - ✓ A $60 million fine, the proceeds of which were to go toward an endowment for preventing child abuse. According to the NCAA, this was the equivalent of a typical year's gross revenue from the football program. The NCAA specified that Penn State cannot cut other sports programs or scholarships to pay this penalty.
  - ✓ Five years probation
  - ✓ A four-year post-season ban
  - ✓ Vacating of all wins from 1998 to 2011—that's 112 wins in all. This had the effect of stripping the Nittany Lions of their shared Big Ten titles in 2005 and 2008. It also removed 111 wins from Paterno's record, dropping him from first to 12th on the NCAA's all-time wins list

✓ Loss of a total of 40 initial scholarships from 2013 to 2017. During the same period, Penn State is limited to 65 total scholarships, only two more than a Division I FCS (formerly I-AA) school is allowed.

✓ Penn State was required to adopt all recommendations for reform delineated in the Freeh report.

✓ Penn State must enter into an "athletics integrity agreement" with the NCAA and Big Ten, appoint a university-wide athletic compliance officer and compliance council, and accept an NCAA-appointed athletic integrity monitor for the duration of its probation.

✓ The NCAA President Mark Emmert stated that the sanctions were levied "not to be just punitive, but to make sure the university establishes an athletic culture and daily mindset in which football will never again be placed ahead of education, nurturing and protecting young people."

• Penn State's regional accreditation was put on "warning" status.

• The Big Ten Conference subsequently imposed an additional $13 million fine.

- Numerous additional civil lawsuits are ongoing.
  At the time of this writing, Penn State University
  has tentative settlements totaling $60 million.
  However, this figure does not cover every claim
  made, and it is expected that the trustees will
  be asked to approve more when other tentative
  agreements are reached.

As in all situations, there are costs, such as those
listed above, that can easily be tallied and quantified.
However, sometimes the highest price is one that can't
be calculated. In the Penn State scandal, many people
who are being punished had no say in the decisions
made. Obviously—and most importantly—a number
of young boys, now men, have been damaged by the
abuse to which they were subjected. The actions of the
perpetrators and those who were responsible for protecting them have left these men with childhoods they
can't recapture, distrust of the very system that should
have protected them, and scars that may never heal.

Other consequences must also be acknowledged:
the loss of reputation for the university; loss of confidence of those alums who now have to answer for the
actions of the institution; the small and large businesses (hotels, restaurants, concession sales) that count on

crowds at athletic events; student athletes whose career hopes have diminished; and even the loss of revenue for the university. Parents don't want to send their kids to a university that allows crimes against children.

As you can see, the list of consequences goes on and on, all because of the actions of a few leaders who were not willing to hold others accountable or, more importantly, hold *themselves* accountable for doing the right thing.

At Penn State, many people were badly damaged by the behavior of one individual (Sandusky), and by the lack of action by the university leaders (Paterno, Spanier, and Curley). Had the university officials done the right thing from the beginning—held Sandusky accountable—many people would have been spared, including themselves.

Let's not forget the Hillsboro football incident we mentioned earlier. This is an extreme case of the cost of unaccountability. How do you put a price tag on that debacle? Ninety-six people lost their lives and several hundred were injured.

Families of the deceased spent twenty years fighting to clear the names of their loved ones.

Thankfully, most of us will never be involved in such high-stakes crises. Still, we are each given daily opportunities to hold ourselves accountable and to hold others accountable. Our choices make all the difference.

PART THREE

PART THREE

WHY THEY FOLLOW

ACCOUNTABILITY AND CULTURE

As above, so below

—Brian Bedford

For accountability to *take*—for it to be part of the success of an organization—it has to be ingrained in that organization's culture. So before we continue, let's first make sure we have a common understanding of what culture is, and how accountability affects it.

How do you define culture? To us, culture means the customs, beliefs, individual actions, and patterns of behavior of a particular group at a particular time. Culture is everywhere. Every country has its own culture. Companies have their own cultures. Even families have distinct cultures. Culture dictates which behaviors are expected, encouraged, and rewarded, and which are punished. People typically describe their own culture as "the way we do things around here."

Sometimes a culture develops over time; other times it can be carefully planned and managed. Take corporate culture. Many companies have their core values posted on the office walls or on their websites, and some even give training courses to help employees behave in accordance with the culture. All of this may help, but it doesn't make a culture. Culture isn't determined by what we *say*, but by what we *do*. The behaviors and actions that are allowed, encouraged, and rewarded determine—and reflect—the culture.

Brian's favorite saying is "As above, so below." What he means is that people look to their leaders— parents, coaches, bosses—to see how they behave and they follow their lead. "As above, so below."

To illustrate, we worked in an organization that had a very formal leader. He always wore a jacket and tie, and of course this drove the dress code for the entire organization. There was nothing written—formal dress was just understood. Later the company underwent a transition to a new leader, and this man was informal. He never wore a jacket and tie, and guess what? Within days of his taking over, all the men stopped wearing jackets and ties. Again, nothing was written. It just happened. This illustrates the ever-evolving nature of corporate culture. It can change for many reasons—especially when leadership changes.

Every time leaders make decisions, they signal what is important to the organization. They make clear what the corporate values are. How do we treat each other? Which behaviors get rewarded, and which have negative consequences? How do we treat our customers?

Incentives, rewards, and consequences play a huge role in setting or defining the culture. Incentives and rewards can reinforce the kind of behavior we want repeated or encouraged. That's pretty obvious. If we do certain things, and get encouragement from our leaders, we are likely to keep doing these things. In other words, there are incentives for making the right choices—sometimes those incentives include bonuses and promotions.

Conversely, consequences let people know what is not accepted in the culture. Generally, we aren't so good at this side of things, and often we're guilty of making all sorts of excuses to avoid an honest, straightforward conversation about what needs to be improved. Many people don't want to hear feedback, and even fewer people want to give it.

Later in these pages, we'll introduce you to a process that will help you with giving feedback, a vital component of holding people accountable. Giving feedback is critical for a leader who wants to hold his or her people accountable. Ideally, when a leader tells someone that an action or behavior is inappropriate, that person will learn and will alter future behavior. Sometimes, though, consequences have to be applied to drive the message home. In business that may be accomplished by withholding increases or declining to award a promotion or a bonus.

Accountability is also established through incentives, rewards, and consequences, but the people being rewarded or punished are not the only ones impacted. Onlookers to this process learn from what they see. If they witness rewards and recognition, they, too, can alter their behavior in hopes of getting similar rewards.

The same thing happens with consequences; people will understand what actions and attitudes limit success, and they will modify their behavior accordingly. So holding employees accountable, or failing to do so, can yield compounded results for the benefit, or the detriment, of the organization.

Think about the organizations you are aware of that have something in their core values about treating employees with respect. There are plenty of them out there. You may see something about this on their websites or on plaques on the wall. Now we'd like to introduce you to one of their managers, Good Ol' Joe. Not all is good with Good Ol' Joe. He's the guy that always gets away with behavior that is inconsistent with those core values.

You all know Good Ol' Joe. He always gets the job done. You need some extra sales to meet the target for the quarter? Joe's your man. However, Good Ol' Joe always leaves blood and bones behind him in the process. He's rude to his peers, he only works on what is important to him, and he yells at and intimidates his employees. You get the idea. And, by the way, Good Ol' Joe has a colleague, Jane, who is just as bad. This is not a male-only issue!

Sadly, Good Ol' Joe is not the only problem in this scenario. His boss is just as much to blame, maybe more so. Where is the accountability? As long as Joe delivers the numbers, his boss is happy, so he doesn't deal with Joe's behavior, and if Joe isn't held accountable, he assumes that what he is doing is okay, and he keeps right on doing it.

What do other employees take from this? It's not hard to know, is it? Others soon infer that all this culture stuff on the website or on the walls is meaningless, because all that matters is the bottom line. To behave like Joe is to reach success. Exit accountability, and with it the very culture the business is looking for.

We want to drive home the point that in order to build accountability in your chosen space, you have to embed it consistently into your culture. It's all about setting clear expectations, giving feedback, and managing rewards and consequences. These are the steps that will ensure the performance outcomes you desire. Relying only on individuals isn't enough, even though strong leaders are needed to help make this possible. For a culture of accountability to thrive, you must have systems and processes built in to ensure its success.

WHY THE FIX?

WHY INSTALL AN ACCOUNTABILITY CULTURE?

Accountability breeds response-ability.

—Stephen R. Covey, *The Seven Habits of Highly Effective People*

I f culture is made up of behaviors and actions of the people in an organization, it only follows that it is something that can be created, managed, or changed. Having a culture that is supportive of your strategy, as well as the work you are trying to accomplish, will make it easier for you to be successful. You wouldn't imagine trying to be successful as an organization without the right people, with the right skills and abilities, or without having the tools and processes in place. A supportive culture is every bit as important to your success.

In a new organization, one that doesn't have set processes, or an established "way we do it around here," a culture is much easier to set on the right course. The culture can be established from the beginning of the organization and carefully guided into what the organization needs to be successful.

An existing organization, by contrast, has a culture that took a long time to be created, so it is likely to take some time and much effort to change. Oftentimes an unsupportive culture is a huge part of what makes the organization unsuccessful. Notice how often, when a new CEO arrives in a company, or a new coach arrives in a sports team, they talk about the need to "change the culture around here." However, just changing the CEO or top leader isn't enough to change an ingrained culture overnight.

That said, there are certain things that can change quickly if the organization sees it in its best interest. We call these quick wins. Like the example we gave you earlier, in which the new CEO didn't wear a jacket and tie. Most people prefer a more casual dress code, so as soon as they saw the CEO dressed more casually, boom: dress code changed. However, in a more established culture, and when the required changes are perceived to be less desirable, it may take a lot of hard work and patience to see them through. After all, we are all creatures of habit, and change is hard for us. But once people understand what is expected, and realize that there are incentives for holding themselves accountable and holding others accountable, they will begin to see the benefits of the new culture. Then others will get on board, and change will accelerate.

Since building an accountability-based culture involves time and effort, you might ask, "Why should we bother? What's in it for us?" Good questions. Here are some of the major benefits we see in an accountability-based culture.

BENEFITS

- Employees are more likely to be open and honest about issues, so that issues can be resolved. This goes hand in hand with the idea that organizations that don't want to hear the truth become organizations that can't tell the truth.
- You're much less likely to have major issues take you by surprise. Major issues arise when minor ones go unaddressed.
- When employees say they'll do something, they can be relied on to do it. Trust strengthens relationships and makes for a more cohesive workplace.
- Employees are more likely to be supportive of one another, the team, and the overall company objectives.
- Employees share honest feedback.
- Other companies' customers, vendors, and partners will want to do business with you because they know you can be relied upon and trusted.
- Bottom line—you'll be more successful!

In all our various consulting assignments, one common theme from leaders and Human Resources professionals is that they spend an inordinate amount of time on the least effective members of an organization, addressing issues of performance, attendance, attitude, and conflicts between employees. This means they don't spend enough time coaching and supporting the top performers, on whom the company's success depends. Creating an accountability-focused workforce will have the benefit of addressing that imbalance. Accountable employees could address these issues directly with one another—freeing up leaders to spend time with high potential employees and to focus on more strategic issues.

As an example, our friend Kerri works in a company with a very strong culture of accountability. Here's what she has to say about it.

> I was introduced to a concept here called "the accountability tunnel." It's when you are about to recommend an action be taken by the organization, or when you are about to take sole responsibility for completion of a crucial task. I was asked whether I was prepared to enter the accountability tunnel. At first, I didn't understand what the president of the company meant, but after we talked

about it I knew that he was asking me if I was prepared enough to make this recommendation and to deal with any and all consequences of that recommendation. By challenging me early on, the president made it very clear what his expectations were, that my recommendation was very important and others were going to rely on it. And if I needed more time, that was completely acceptable—making the right recommendation was the most important outcome. By making my decision, I was acknowledging to the team that I accepted responsibility. Also, when others enter the tunnel, we as colleagues know what a big deal that is so their recommendation/ opinion/statement naturally bears more weight and we listen more intently. The accountability tunnel is brought up only a few times a year but it's such a big deal when it is that the concept naturally breeds day-to-day accountability in more routine actions. In other words, accountability is just part of our culture.

Wouldn't you like to have employees that understand the weight of their decisions the way Kerri does? Can you imagine how successful your organization could be if all employees were this accountable for their work?

PART FOUR

PART FOUR

What's the Fix?

How to Install an Accountability Culture

If something is worth doing, it's worth doing right.

—Les Miller, Julie's father

We have a proven process for putting accountability front and center. The process is straightforward, but don't mistake that for easy. It isn't. Installing a culture requires focus, time, and commitment, and if you're not prepared to invest these things in the process, don't even start. A half-hearted approach to installing a culture is worse than no approach at all; it's the quickest way to disillusion your team. As Julie's dad has been telling her all her life, "If something is worth doing, it's worth doing right."

Now what you've all been waiting for, how to fix your accountability issues! Here's our four-step process to help you build a stronger and more effective business through creating your unique culture of accountability.

MILLERBEDFORD'S FOUR STEPS TO ACCOUNTABILITY

1. Share your accountability vision
2. Bring accountability to life
3. Weave accountability into the fabric of your organization
4. Model the way

1. Share Your Accountability Vision

If you've read to here, we're assuming that accountability is important to you. Maybe you're starting a business, and you want to build a solid foundation of accountability from the ground up. Or maybe you've taken over, or moved up in, an organization in which accountability is lacking, and you want to fix it. Or perhaps you just want to give your kids a solid grounding of accountability.

In all these cases, *you* have in your mind why accountability is important. Now you must get everyone else to share your vision and have the same level of commitment to it that you do.

To get everyone's attention, you need a short, strong, convincing statement of the value that an accountability-based culture creates. You need to know, and be able to say, why it's of importance to the success of your particular organization, so that you can share it consistently, at every opportunity. This is what is referred to as an elevator speech—clear, to-the-point, and easy to deliver in a short span of time, such as when you're riding in an elevator with someone.

Your elevator speech should answer the following questions:

- What problem are we trying to fix?
- Why is accountability important to us?
- What do we need you to do differently?
- What benefits will we see if our organization builds an accountability-based culture?

Your speech might go something like this: "You know that accountability is of prime importance to me. Lately we've been missing our targets, our customers are upset, and instead of being accountable for our mistakes, we're busy making excuses. That needs to stop NOW! We need to take ownership of our problems early and get issues fixed before they impact our customers. When we do this, everything gets better for all of us. Our business grows and we are more successful."

2. Bring Accountability to Life

It's important that all employees share a clear understanding of what accountability means in the organization, so that all employees, no matter who they are or what they do, understand clearly how they are expected to behave. One way to ensure that, to *bring the vision of accountability to life* for all involved, is to develop behavior statements that help clarify the vision. The statements will answer the fundamental question of what, precisely, we are trying to fix, implement, or eliminate. This is especially helpful in international companies, because accountability might mean different things in different countries, languages, and cultures.

Consider the following examples:

Accountability Behavior Statements

- Always do what you say you'll do.
- If you are going to miss a commitment,

communicate that as soon as you can, to all who need to know.

- Take responsibility for your mistakes, as well as for your successes.
- Always tell the truth.
- Bring issues up as you discover them.
- Provide honest feedback to whoever needs to hear it, as soon as concerns arise.

Develop a list of *DOs and DON'Ts* to ensure clarity. This helps individuals know exactly what they *should do* and what they *should not do.*

DOs might include:

- Do have a clear understanding of your role and responsibilities.
- Do be open, honest, and truthful.
- Do surface issues to appropriate people.
- Do recommend solutions to problems.

As for DON'Ts:

- Don't blame others.
- Don't make excuses.
- Don't hope someone else will bring up the problem.

Once the behavior statements are complete, take every opportunity to communicate them. We encourage our client companies to put together a communication roll-out strategy that includes posters, screen savers, badge stickers, and anything else that will get the word out for all to see and internalize. You can never over-communicate your core values and behaviors!

3. Weave Accountability into the Fabric of the Organization

Now you need to make sure that accountability "sticks" across the organization. How do you do that? We say you weave it into the fabric of the organization. The idea is to link accountability to all the systems and processes you already have in place. Recruiting and Selection, Performance Management, Rewards and Succession Planning, Communication, Training and Development, and New Employee Orientation should all consistently reinforce the importance of accountability. Some examples.

Recruiting and Selection - It's much easier to hire employees with an accountability mindset than to train them. Harder yet is the process of getting rid of employees who aren't accountable. Successful leaders remain involved in the hiring process, and more and more companies are using assessment tools to make sure that prospective employees have the traits and behaviors they're looking for. We recommend adding behaviorally based questions to the interview process, to ensure you are hiring the proper candidates. A few good questions might be:

- If I asked your boss how you demonstrated accountability, what example would he or she give?
- Share with me a time where you made a big mistake and how you handled it.
- Summarize a difficult conversation you had with an employee who had failed to meet a commitment.
- Describe a situation in which you very clearly held others accountable for their performance and it paid off. How did you do this and what was the outcome?

Performance Management – Employees need to know that they will be responsible not only for the *results* of their work, but also for how they go about their work, and that their rewards will depend on both. The

Accountability Behavior Statements and the *DOs and DON'Ts* you created could be added to the performance review and help drive discussions with employees on how they are incorporating them.

Rewards and Succession Planning – Promotions and salary increases should only be considered for people who demonstrate accountability as defined by the organization. When your employees do well, reward and promote them. If they don't do well, apply consequences and make sure they understand that their performance will limit their success and possible progression. Needless to say, an employee who doesn't demonstrate accountability should not be listed in a succession plan.

Communication – Do you hold regular communications meetings with your team or organization? We recommend it, because meetings provide an opportunity for management to highlight people who have demonstrated good accountability; to show where things went wrong; and to analyze what could have been done better. This should be done in a way that instructs rather than punishes. Use every available communication tool to emphasize why accountability is important: electronic signs, business reviews, one-on-one meetings, e-mails, posters, and more. If, by way of regular communication, you reinforce the changes you want to see, you will drive the value deep into the organization.

Training and Development –

Develop a training plan that teaches all employees:

- why accountability is important and how to understand accountability behaviors;
- how their accountability mindset and behaviors will affect their pay and progression in the organization; and
- how to provide feedback to one another, since this is essential to developing a culture of accountability.

Develop a training plan that teaches all organization leaders what their role is as accountability role models.

Make sure to add this to the *New Employee Orientation*, so that new employees can be successful immediately!

4. Model the Way

Okay, now you've done the easy part. This last piece is much harder, and it's the reason so many culture processes fail. Too often, leaders don't demonstrate the behaviors they have declared to be essential to the organization, nor do they hold others accountable to them. Employees are cynics, and they're suspicious, often rightly, of the fine words they see and hear. They're always watching and waiting for any sign that proves leadership isn't really on board with all the accountability culture stuff. If they see the disconnect, your culture initiative will be dead in the water.

We would suggest that all successful culture changes have something in common: leaders who apply the relentless focus, time, and commitment necessary to build the required culture, and who themselves serve as role models for the required behaviors. You've heard us say, "As above, so below." In the end, the establishment of a culture is all about how leaders behave, and what behaviors they reward and discourage. In other words, establishment of a culture requires strong and consistent leadership.

In order to **Model the Way,** leaders should follow this process:

Hold Yourself Accountable

You must hold yourself accountable to at least the same level of expectation you have for your employees. In other words, "Walk the talk." Know that everyone is going to be watching you and everything starts at the top. You must set the example that others will follow.

Set Clear Expectations

Without clear expectations, there's no way to hold someone accountable. By *bringing accountability to life* you define the *accountability behaviors statements and DOs and DON'Ts* for your organization. You must make sure that each employee has a clear understanding of what these mean in the job he or she performs.

Hold Others Accountable

Let's get back to the basics here. You have to

tell your employees the truth. You can't do this without having conversations with people about what they are doing well and where they need to improve. This is where the accountability process seems to break down most often. Don't let that happen to you.

Provide Feedback

Once you have trained your employee on your expectations, the best way to hold them accountable is to provide regular feedback on their performance, so now comes our lecture on feedback.

FEEDBACK

What we find in nearly all companies and all industries (and also in parents) is that no one likes to give feedback—especially constructive feedback. Most people aren't good at it, so they don't do it! This includes very senior managers and leaders.

We have a friend named Jan who's a personal business coach. We mentioned to her that many managers are reluctant to provide feedback to employees. She was a bit surprised by that. Weeks later, we got together and she told us that she had decided to test our assumption. When having a conversation with the CEO of a company regarding one of his employees (his employee is Jan's client), the CEO mentioned deficits in the employee's skills and abilities that he deemed were keeping this employee from being successful. Jan asked, "Have you had a conversation with the employee about these issues?" to which the CEO responded, "No." Jan was shocked, but after she coached the CEO on how to share feedback with his employee, and after he delivered the feedback—no surprise here—the employee's performance improved!

Realistically, most employees expect feedback, especially from their managers. It's the only way they know whether their performance is on target—and let's face it, without feedback to the contrary, most of us assume we are meeting expectations. Wouldn't our bosses tell us otherwise?

Feedback is a way to keep employees moving in the right direction. Leaders can encourage the behavior and actions they want and discourage those they don't.

Employees benefit from this feedback if they are willing to receive the input and make improvements to their performance. These course corrections will help the employee progress faster than those who are unwilling to heed the suggestions. Yes, sometimes it's uncomfortable to hear feedback and learn of our deficiencies, but as Sheryl Sandberg points out in her book *Lean In*, "The upside of painful knowledge is so much greater than the downside of blissful ignorance." So employees should view feedback as a gift rather than a punishment. In fact, the best employees make it a practice to ask for feedback, because after all, sharing feedback is very hard and made much easier if it is requested.

Since sharing feedback is so difficult, here are some pointers. For feedback to be productive, it is helpful to share feedback regularly and without delay. If this practice becomes part of the culture, others will come to expect it and not feel that it's anything unusual. Leaders should share impressions as soon as they see the behavior they would like to encourage or discourage. Make sure feedback is specific, focusing on the particular issue or behavior in question. If a leader will focus on what the person actually said or did— the facts and nothing but the facts—without labeling the employee or the action, the employee will be more likely to hear and heed the feedback.

> **Feedback should be:**
> - Shared regularly, without delay
> - Expected or asked for by employees
> - Specific
> - Focused on the facts
> - Considered as a gift

Which of the following approaches do you think has the greater chance of starting a quality conversation with your employee?

"You said you would get the report filed by yesterday, and you missed your commitment." or

"You're lazy and always screwing up. Once again you proved I can't count on you."

We know what we'd respond to better. In the first approach, your judgmental comments are left out of the situation—you shared only the facts; judgment can spark a conflict and lead to debate. You may feel better initially trying it the second way, but such language doesn't solve the problem; in fact it makes it worse. If you repeat exactly the words your employee chose or the actions he or she took, the facts are inarguable.

When Julie was in graduate school, she learned this model from Ben Strickland and Cathy Geddie, and it's one that has worked well in her career. It's called

S.I.S. Feedback, which stands for Situation, Impact, Suggestion. It works like this:

Situation – **"When you...**

- Describe the situation
- What did the person say or do?

Impact - **"It is good because, or it was bad because...**

- Describe what impact it had.

Suggestion – **"What I would like you to do in the future..."**

- Suggest ways to continue this, or stop this.

So in the situation above, your conversation with your employee might go like this:

Situation

"When you failed to get the report filed by the deadline you committed to...

Impact

...you caused a delay in the process, which resulted in other team members having to scramble and work overtime to meet our company's target.

Suggestion

...In the future, I expect you to meet your commitments, or let me know in advance if you can't."

Likewise, if you want to provide positive reinforcement, your message could sound like this...

Situation

"When you consistently meet your commitments,

Impact

...it lets the whole team know that they can count on you.

Suggestion

...Keep up the good work!"

This is actually a very straightforward process, and it's easy to remember. But people are uncomfortable giving feedback, so they sometimes find it difficult to put into practice. We teach a practical session on S.I.S. feedback in our leadership classes, and we are often surprised how even experienced leaders struggle with it.

Giving feedback is a vital component of a leader's job; difficult or not, it has to be done. Practice makes perfect!

When Julie was working as an HR manager at Motorola, she consulted with a manager about a very long-tenured employee we'll call Jim. Jim was being paid a higher salary than his performance justified, and he was in jeopardy of being placed on a performance improvement plan (PIP). Julie asked the manager if Jim was capable of meeting the expectations of the PIP, to which the manager said, "No, he really is at the end of his career and doesn't have the skills, or enough time left in his career, to be successful."

Julie asked, "Why, then, are we going to the effort to put this elaborate plan together, if we feel he won't be successful? Why don't we downgrade him to a position he can be more confident with and allow him to end his career feeling good about himself rather than a failure?"

The manager's response was interesting, "I don't think we've ever downgraded anyone before. Won't he be offended?"

To which Julie said, "We won't know unless we ask, but certainly, how will he feel if we put him on a path where he has zero chance to be successful?"

Julie took this situation as a opportunity. She scheduled a meeting with Jim, just to talk to him about how things were with his job. He said, "Actually, my job is very stressful. My health hasn't been as good as it used to be and the stress isn't helping."

Julie asked if anyone had ever talked to him about his performance, and he said, "No, in fact, people don't really talk to me at all. They seem to be avoiding me."

Julie told Jim that after a conversation with his boss she learned that he wasn't really performing at the level expected for his grade level and salary, and that she didn't think anyone wanted to tell him that for fear of hurting his feelings. She discussed with him the possibility of downgrading him to a different position, a job that he had performed well in the past. Julie informed Jim that this would require a reduction of his salary over time, as outlined in company policy. She told him that the choice was his: remain in his current position and try to meet a more demanding set of expectations, or accept the alternate position.

Julie encouraged Jim to think about his options over the weekend and come back to talk to her. The following week, he came to Julie's office with a big smile on his face, looking as if his load had been lifted. Julie says she will never forget what he said. "Julie, I want to shake your hand and thank you for being honest with me. I knew something was wrong, I could feel the stress, but I had no idea what was wrong. No one was willing to tell me the truth, until you."

To this day, this conversation still brings tears to Julie's eyes. Didn't this long-serving employee deserve the truth? Didn't he deserve to be treated like an adult, and to have all the information he needed to make important decisions for his life? Jim accepted the downgrade and always had a smile and wave for Julie when she saw him at work.

Sharing feedback is not easy, but telling the truth is part of what being accountable means. This is a part of what is expected, whether you are a business leader, a parent, or whatever your role is.

There are sometimes tough decisions to be made, and how you face up to those will determine how successful you will be in the long run.

In applying the above four steps, the absolute commitment of the leadership of the organization is vital. The organization will be watching to see if leadership *does* what it *says*, not just in the short term, but also for the long haul. Leadership decisions and actions will be analyzed according to how they measure up to this behavior, and exceptions will be seen as a lack of commitment to the process.

Many companies can implement a process like this, but only the truly successful ones are able to keep it going over time. This is not a sprint; it's a marathon. To be successful requires sustained focus and relentless dedication by the leadership.

So ask yourself what values and behaviors are important to you? How do you want your company to be perceived, your employees to perform? How do you want your kids to behave? You'll be doing all of them a favor by instilling an accountability mindset.

PART FIVE

WITH TENACIOUS FOCUS!

ACCOUNTABILITY IN ACTION: A REAL-LIFE EXAMPLE

The most important quality I look for in a player is accountability. You've got to be accountable for who you are. It's too easy to blame things on someone else.

—Lenny Wilkens, former NBA basketball coach

In these pages, we've talked about why accountability is important, what disasters can befall when accountability is absent, and the benefits that spring from an accountability-based culture, whether in business, sports, or families. Finally, we have outlined the steps necessary to make accountability stick.

We'd like to finish by giving an example of accountability in action, to demonstrate how successful an organization can become when it's built on such a foundation. A sterling example of this success is Manchester United, one of the world's great soccer clubs, and its coach, Sir Alex Ferguson, who retired from his position at the end of the 2012-2013 season.

SAF, to use the U.K. media shorthand for Sir Alex, was the longest-tenured coach of any major soccer club in the world, and he won more major trophies than any current coach in Europe. When we study his career, we note that his success was built on a number of critical factors—his emphasis on youth development as a source of talent, rather than simply buying and selling players, for example—but from our perspective, one of his most important gifts as a leader was the way he held himself and his players accountable. He might not put it that way himself (we haven't talked to him), but his emphasis on accountability comes out loud and clear in everything he does.

Ferguson believed that no one person, including himself, was more important than the institution of

Manchester United, and he held everyone to that standard. No matter how popular or skillful a player might be, if he didn't measure up to the standards SAF set, or if SAF felt that the player's presence was a distraction to the team as a whole, he held that player accountable, and—unless his behavior changed—the player was gone.

When Sir Alex first arrived at United in 1986, the team was not being managed to his standards. There wasn't enough emphasis on fitness, stars weren't being held accountable for consistent performance, and the club had turned a blind eye to the significant drinking that was going on among members of the team. All that changed with Ferguson's arrival. He emphasized the importance of fitness and discipline, and he established a culture where everyone, whether a star player or a cleaner in the locker room, was treated the same. To show that he was serious, several star players who, although popular with the fans, didn't measure up to his standards, were let go. His view was that talent is great, but it needs to be supported by hard work, and a player who wasn't prepared to work hard would soon find himself out of a job, no matter how talented.

Sir Alex maintained these high standards on

a consistent basis over his twenty-six years with Manchester United. Examples of his "no one is bigger than the club" ethic involved some of the biggest names in the club's history, such as:

- Roy Keane, for many years an inspirational club captain and a fan idol, who made the mistake of criticizing his fellow players in public. Gone.
- Ruud van Nistelrooy, one of the most prolific goal scorers of Ferguson's career, talked publicly about the possibility of moving to another club. Gone.
- David Beckham, who became a distraction as a media star, especially after his marriage to one of the Spice Girls. Gone.

These actions are examples of SAF's holding people accountable to his view that no individual is more important than the club, no matter how popular, no matter how talented. It also explains why, over the twenty-six years the coach was at United, the club never had to deal with the major scandals or stories of locker room unrest that routinely afflicted other clubs. That's not to say that issues didn't arise; when you have young players earning millions, things are going to happen. When players violated SAF's standards, he dealt with them forcefully—but internally. A famous comment of his from a 2009 speech at Trinity College, Dublin, was "You can't ever lose control—not when you're dealing with millionaires. If anyone steps out of my control, that's them dead." This approach allowed him to manage temperamental thoroughbreds who might otherwise have created mayhem.

SAF was quick to hold himself accountable to high standards, too. When United lost the Premier League title, by the narrowest of margins, at the end of the 2012 season, he blamed himself, not the players. And when the team exited from the Champions' League (the competition he held in the highest regard of all) at an early stage in the same season, he blamed his own team selections and tactics. In a February 2013 BBC interview, he fixed the interviewer with a steely look after a question on the 2012 league campaign and said, "That will not happen again. I'll make sure of it." And it didn't. Manchester United were champions again in 2013.

In common with that, on-field mistakes by players were dealt with in private as well. SAF never harshly criticized players in public. He might have said a player "could have done better," or "perhaps made a mistake," but you would never hear him throwing an individual player under the bus. The team, yes; individuals, no. And very often the spirit of accountability he created at the club ensured that the players held one another accountable on his behalf.

One of the great players developed and nurtured under SAF's youth development plan, Gary Neville, who captained United for many years, put it like this on Sky TV recently:

> There's an incredible amount of accountability in that dressing room. It's not a place that's forgiving; it's a place where you get people who will confront each other after mistakes are made. If you play at that club, in that dressing room, under that manager, it's about learning fast. (Sky TV, Jan. 22, 2013)

One last thing for which SAF held himself, as well as his players, accountable: he hated to lose, never knew when he was beaten, and never gave up. His United teams showed this characteristic all the time; they fought until the end, and they were famous for their end-of-game heroics. The most perfect example is the 1999 European Champions Cup final, when they looked down-and-out against Bayern Munich, but scored two goals in the last three minutes to win the game.

So, let's take a look at SAF and Manchester United in the context of our **MillerBedford Four Steps to Accountability** process. Although the playing side of Manchester United is not a business, in the traditional sense that major corporations are businesses, with formalized systems and processes for recruitment, selection, performance management, and employee communications, many things that SAF did are exactly in line with our "Four Steps" process.

Step 1: Share Your Accountability Vision

SAF did this from day one. The club is all-important; no one is bigger than the club; people who don't behave in accordance with the standards SAF required were not kept.

Step 2: Bring Accountability to Life

We're sure SAF didn't have a list of **DOs and DON'Ts** on his wall! But if you look at the things he did over the years, most of them follow the same pattern. You can list the elements:

DOs

- Do take responsibility for your mistakes.
- Do provide honest feedback.
- Do understand your roles and responsibilities.

DON'Ts

- Don't blame others.

Although he didn't use these exact words (his ideas were usually more colorfully expressed, and in a broad Scottish accent!), these principles can be found in his interviews, books, and speeches. And we'd be willing to bet his players understood them perfectly!

Step 3: Weave Accountability into the Fabric of the Organization

As we've said, United is a soccer club, and the playing side doesn't have all the systems and processes that exist in businesses. Nevertheless, when you look at the major systems we talk about, such as Recruiting and Selection, Performance Management,

Rewards, Communication, and Training/Development, you see that, under SAF's leadership, accountability within the club was built into every stage. Players who fit the mold were hired; they were given feedback on performance, and held accountable for mistakes; and they were rewarded with raises and new contracts when they did well. Communication took place all the time, with team talks before, during, and after games, and training was a critical building block in the success of the team. In fact, many businesses could benefit by taking a good look at the way successful coaches manage their teams!

Step 4:   Model the Way

This is where organizations frequently fail, and in Manchester United, SAF was the model—his actions aligned with his words. He set clear expectations, gave feedback against those expectations, and took action when performance didn't measure up.

Accountability does make organizations more successful. Alex Ferguson was the most successful and longest-serving manager in Manchester United history.

During his leadership, Manchester United won:

- 13 English Premier League Titles
- 2 European Champions' League Crowns
- 5 Football Association Cups
- 4 League Cups

Under his leadership, and because of his focus on accountability, Manchester United has become one of the wealthiest sports franchises in the world. According to Forbes Magazine's 2013 listing, the club is valued at over $3 billion. Accountability isn't just an important principle; it can also have a very positive impact on the bottom line.

WANT TO FIX?
SUMMARY

My main job was developing talent. I was a gardener providing water and other nourishment to our top 750 people. Of course, I had to pull out some weeds, too.

—Jack Welch, Former CEO of General Electric

I n these pages, we've shown you the good, the bad, and the ugly of accountability. We hope that by now you can see that accountability is good for a business and that it really does help breed success. But as we've said many times throughout our book, this stuff is hard. Holding yourself accountable is hard. Holding others accountable is hard. Giving feedback is hard, and so is receiving feedback. Add to that the fact that anyone being held accountable who doesn't like it can easily post negative comments through all the outlets offered by social media these days. It's difficult to avoid the question, why bother? It obviously is not the easiest path to take, so why expose yourself to all the added grief to install an accountability culture?

Maybe you see accountability as a path for you to be more successful at work. Maybe you just want to have a reputation as someone who can always be trusted to act with integrity. Or maybe it's more personal for you—you just want to be able to sleep well at night having the satisfaction of knowing you did the right thing.

All of these are great reasons but they don't really get to the reason you may be willing to expend the effort required to ensure accountability. It's not as if there is some grand cosmic reward for behaving in an accountable fashion. We have thought about this a lot, and from our perspective there are two compelling reasons. The first revolves around success. Our experience shows that individuals who hold themselves accountable are also much more likely to be successful. Families that focus on accountability function better and are much less likely to have problems than those that don't, and the children from these families have a much greater chance of being successful in life. Organizations that focus on accountability are much more successful than those that don't.

Our second compelling reason revolves around hope. We all hope for a better world in which to live. We hope to pass on to today's children a world in which they can rely on others, and we hope to offer a way to bring them up so that others can rely on them.

Remember the story we told you at the beginning of the book, about the airplane captain who stepped out of the cockpit to deliver the bad news that we were all boarded on the wrong plane? Because we continued to think about him as we wrote this book, we decided to track him down to find out what caused him to behave in such an accountable fashion that day.

We asked him what made him stand face-to-face with us, in the aisle of the plane, over the public address system to deliver the message rather than stay in the cockpit. He said, "I always do that kind of thing when things go wrong." He contemplated further about why he tended to handle bad news in that manner and said, "When I was a boy, if I screwed up—and I screwed up quite a bit—my dad used to bring me into the living room to explain myself. I couldn't look at my feet; I had to look at him squarely in the eyes to explain myself. As a boy it was really tough, but as I got older, I realized people liked the personal delivery. They could tell that I was being sincere and I'm more comfortable looking in their eyes so I can get their reaction." He went on, "I'm *so* grateful to my dad for this lesson. It was much easier to learn that lesson at an early age. Whether I'm dealing with a peer or a customer, whether delivering good news or bad, face-to-face is so much better than an e-mail or even being in the cockpit."

In closing we would like to direct our questions to you since, after all, you have to find your own guiding truth. Is this unaccountable world the kind of world in which you want to live or raise your children? Do you have the toughness and strength of character, as our captain's father did, to ingrain that behavior in others? Just by raising his son to look people in the eyes and behave in an accountable fashion he made a huge difference in the world. It would be hard to know how many people are positively impacted by the captain, but we certainly were that day.

Are you doing everything you can to hold yourself and others accountable? Of course it's not easy. If it were, more people would be doing it. Few worthwhile things in life are easy. But living an accountable life, and influencing others to do the same, can bring huge benefits to you personally and professionally, and we sure *hope* you will do it! The first time you take that brave step to hold yourself or someone else accountable and receive accolades you'll know you are on the right track.

We are here to applaud you and support you any way we can. We wish you every success in making this a more accountable world, and we're counting on you!

We'd love to be involved in your journey. You can find us at www.millerbedford.com or via direct e-mail at julie@millerbedford.com, and brian@miller-bedford.com. Please share your stories with us.

We'd enjoy hearing from you!

I'm starting with the man in the mirror
I'm asking him to change his ways
And no message could have been any clearer
If you want to make the world a better place
Take a look at yourself, and then make a change.

—Michael Jackson, "Man in the Mirror"

ACKNOWLEDGEMENTS

As we mentioned in our foreword, the idea of writing a book was a terrifying prospect for us, and the fact that we got through the process relatively unscathed (and without killing each other!) is largely because we were lucky enough to have the help and assistance of some remarkable people, and we'd like to pay tribute to some of them here.

First, our editor, the indefatigable Jan Williams; your grammatical expertise and sense of humor kept us out of trouble on a variety of levels, and your inputs were always valuable. Thanks for never losing patience with us.

Our amazing first readers, Scott Colglazier, Mary McKee, Jewelle Schiedel-Webb and Kerri Scott; your comments and suggestions were hugely helpful, and inspired us to make this book better than it ever had a chance of being without you. We are forever in your debt for all your time and effort.

Our superb book and website design team, Mayapriya Long of Bookwrights, and Al Canton of NewMediaWebsiteDesign.com whose responsiveness, professionalism and humor were a Godsend on many occasions. We couldn't recommend you too highly to anyone putting a book and website together.

Our publicist, Stephanie Barko, who taught these old dogs some new tricks, and forced us to learn about technology in ways we'd never have imagined. Your contacts in the book business were delightful to work with and very professional.

Our airline captain, who gave us the bookends for the book, and inspired us right from the beginning. We're not allowed to name you, but you know who you are. Hopefully we'll be on a plane with you again someday, but a little less drama would be appreciated.

Our friends who encouraged us to write this book in the first place; a big thanks for putting up with our endless book-related conversations and questions, all of which helped mold and shape our thoughts on accountability. You know who you are too!

And last but certainly not least, our cheerleading section, Jan and Les Miller, Julie's parents. Your inexhaustible supply of support and encouragement, not to mention constructive comments, helped us more than you'll ever know. We're sure Lorna and Bill Bedford would have done the same; it's a shame they weren't around to do so. We hope they're reading this somewhere.

If there's anyone we've missed, we apologize, and we'll buy you a glass of wine to make up!

Julie and Brian

INDEX

ABOUT THE AUTHORS

Julie Miller and Brian Bedford first met when they worked together at Motorola, Inc. His final position was Senior Vice President of Human Resources for the Semiconductor Products Sector, an $8 billion business with 50,000 employees, while she finished as Director of Human Resources for the Networking and Computing Systems Group, a $2 billion business within the sector. Brian, born and raised in Dumfries, Scotland, moved to the United States in 1994. Julie is a native Texan, originally from Fort Worth. Today they live in Austin, Texas. (For more information, please visit www.millerbedford.com)

Julie and Brian married in 2000. They knew they had similar professional talents and goals, and that they worked well together. For these reasons, and because they wanted to work as a team, they left the corporate world and, in 2001, established MillerBedford Executive Solutions. In this capacity, Julie and Brian consult with companies to address organizational issues, with specific emphasis on strategy, culture, and leadership. Their extensive business experience allows them to diagnose issues limiting the organization's success, whether strategy, leadership, culture, or capabilities, and then recommend and facilitate solutions.

MillerBedford has worked with companies across multiple disciplines and continents.

They are gifted at helping companies establish a supportive corporate culture that links to and drives the overall organization strategy—and they have a good time doing it. They complement each other well in their presentations and facilitated sessions. Their style is businesslike but informal, focused yet fun. Participants enjoy the sessions and come away informed and ready to contribute to a corporate culture that will lead to success.

Over the past several years, Julie and Brian have noticed a decline in accountability in many companies, as well as in organizations, sports, and even families. Why? And what can be done about it? These questions, and their own step-by-step solution, led Julie and Brian to write this book about what they see as an essential ingredient of successful corporations: a culture of accountability.

In addition to the United States and Canada, Julie and Brian have worked extensively in China, Malaysia, Singapore, Taiwan, all major European countries,

South Africa, and Israel. MillerBedford clients have included Chartered Semiconductor (now part of Global Foundries), ATI (now part of AMD), AMD, Spansion, Lattice Semiconductor, and Kulicke & Soffa.

CPSIA information can be obtained at www.ICGtesting.com
Printed in the USA
LVOW04s1001270814

R8759100001B/R87591PG400824LVX9B/10/P